CO-CBY 612

Meeting Your Goliath

THOMAS S. MONSON

Deseret Book Company
Salt Lake City, Utah

© 1997 Thomas S. Monson

All rights reserved. No part of this book may be reproduced in any form or by any means without permission in writing from the publisher, Deseret Book Company, P. O. Box 30178, Salt Lake City, Utah 84130. This work is not an official publication of The Church of Jesus Christ of Latter-day Saints. The views expressed herein are the responsibility of the author and do not necessarily represent the position of the Church or of Deseret Book Company.

Deseret Book is a registered trademark of Deseret Book Company.

Library of Congress Catalog Card Number 97-76774

ISBN 1-57345-357-9

Printed in the United States of America   72082

10   9   8   7   6   5   4   3   2   1

More than thirty years ago, the stillness of Sinai's desert air was shattered. Jet-powered aircraft streaked toward specified targets, cannons roared, tanks lumbered, men fought and died, women wept, and children cried. The Holy Land, once the personal province of the Prince of Peace, was engulfed by war.

This troubled land has witnessed much conflict throughout its history; its peoples have suffered terrible trials and tribulations. No single battle is better remembered, however, than occurred in the Valley of Elah during the year 1063 B.C. Along the mountains on one side, the feared armies of the Philistines were marshalled to march directly to the heart of Judah and the Jordan Valley. On the other side of the valley, King Saul had drawn up his armies in opposition.

Historians tell us that the opposing forces were about evenly matched in number and in skill. However, the Philistines had managed to keep secret their valued knowledge of smelting and fashioning iron into formidable weapons of war. The sound of hammers pounding upon anvils and the sight of smoke rising skyward from many bellows as the smiths went about the task of sharpening weapons and fashioning new ones must have struck fear into the hearts of Saul's warriors, for even the most novice of soldiers could know the superiority of iron weapons to those of brass.

As often happened when armies faced each other, individual champions challenged others from the opposing forces to single combat. There was considerable precedent for this sort of fighting; and on more than one occasion, notably during the tenure of Samson as judge, battles had been decided by individual combat.

Now, however, the situation was reversed as far as Israel was concerned, and it was a Philistine who dared to challenge all others—a veritable giant of a man called Goliath of Gath. Old accounts tell us that Goliath was ten feet tall. He wore brass armor and a coat of mail. And the staff of his spear would stagger a strong man merely to lift, let alone hurl. His shield was the longest ever seen or heard of, and his sword a fearsome blade.

This champion from the Philistine camp stood and cried unto the armies of Israel, "Why are ye come out to set your battle in array? am not I a Philistine, and ye servants to Saul? choose you a man for you, and let him come down to me."[1]

His challenge was that if he were overpowered by the Israelite warrior, then all the Philistines would become servants to the Israelites. On the other hand, if he were victorious, the Israelites would become their slaves. Goliath roared, "I defy the armies of Israel this day; give me a man, that we may fight together."[2]

And so for forty days came the challenge, met only by fear and trembling. And all the men of Israel, when they saw the man Goliath, "fled from him, and were sore afraid."³

There was one, however, who did not quake with fear nor run in alarm. Rather, he stiffened the spine of Israel's soldiers by his piercing question of rebuke toward them: "Is there not a cause?" Then he said to King Saul, "Let no man's heart fail because of him; thy servant will go and fight with this Philistine."⁴ David, the shepherd boy, had spoken. But he did not speak just as a shepherd boy. For the hands of Samuel, God's prophet, had rested upon his head and anointed him, and the Spirit of the Lord had come upon him.

Saul said to David, "Thou art not able to go against this Philistine to fight with him: for thou art but a youth, and he a man of war from his youth."⁵ But David persevered and, bedecked with the armor of Saul, prepared to meet the giant. Realizing his helplessness while thus garbed, David discarded the armor, took instead his staff in his hand, chose five smooth stones out of the brook, and put them in a shepherd's bag; and with his sling in hand, "he drew near to the Philistine."⁶

All of us remember the shocked exclamation of Goliath: "Am I a dog, that thou comest to me with staves? . . . Come to me, and I will give thy flesh unto the fowls of the air, and to the beasts of the field."⁷

Then David said, "Thou comest to me with a sword, and with a spear, and with a shield: but I come to thee in the name of the

Lord of hosts, the God of the armies of Israel, whom thou hast defied. This day will the Lord deliver thee into mine hand . . . that all the earth may know that there is a God in Israel. And all this assembly shall know that the Lord saveth not with sword and spear: for the battle is the Lord's, and he will give you into our hands."[8]

"And it came to pass, when the Philistine arose, and came and drew nigh to meet David, that David hasted, and ran toward the army to meet the Philistine. And David put his hand in his bag, and took thence a stone, and slang it, and smote the Philistine . . . that the stone sunk into his forehead; and he fell upon his face to the earth. So David prevailed over the Philistine with a sling and with a stone, and smote the Philistine, and slew him."[9]

The battle had thus been fought. The victory had been won. David emerged a national hero, his destiny before him.

Some of us remember David as a shepherd boy divinely commissioned by the Lord through the prophet Samuel. Others of us know him as a mighty warrior; for doesn't the record show the chant of the adoring women following his many victorious battles, "Saul hath slain his thousands, and David his ten thousands"?[10] Or perhaps we look upon him as the inspired poet or as one of Israel's greatest kings. Still others recall that he violated the laws of God and took that which belonged to another—the beautiful Bathsheba. He even arranged the death of her husband, Uriah.

I, however, like to think of David as the righteous lad who

had the courage and the faith to face insurmountable odds when all others hesitated, and to redeem the name of Israel by facing that giant in his life—Goliath of Gath.

Well might we look carefully into our own lives and judge our courage, our faith. Is there a Goliath in your life? Is there one in mine? Does he stand squarely between you and your desired happiness? Oh, your Goliath may not carry a sword or hurl a verbal challenge or insult that all may hear, thus forcing you to decision. He may not be ten feet tall, but he likely will appear equally formidable, and his silent challenge may shame and embarrass.

One man's Goliath may be the stranglehold of a cigarette or perhaps an unquenchable thirst for alcohol. To another, his Goliath may be an unruly tongue or a selfish streak which causes him to spurn the poor and the downtrodden. Envy, greed, fear, laziness, doubt, vice, pride, lust, selfishness, discouragement—all spell Goliath.

The giant you face will not diminish in size nor in power or strength by your vain hoping, wishing, or waiting for him to do so. Rather, he increases in power as his hold upon you tightens. The poet Alexander Pope aptly describes this truth:

> *Vice is a monster of so frightful mien,*
> *As to be hated needs but to be seen;*
> *Yet seen too oft, familiar with her face,*
> *We first endure, then pity, then embrace.*[11]

The battle for our immortal souls is no less important than the battle fought by David. The enemy is no less formidable, the help of Almighty God no farther away. What will our action be? Like David of old, our cause is just. We have been placed upon earth not to fail or fall victim to temptation's snare but rather to succeed. Our giant, our Goliath, must be conquered.

David went to the brook and carefully selected five smooth stones with which he might meet his enemy. He was deliberate in his selection, for there could be no turning back, no second chance; this battle was to be decisive.

Just as David went to the brook, well might we go to our source of supply—the Lord. What polished stones will you select to defeat the Goliath that is robbing you of your happiness by smothering your opportunities? May I offer a few suggestions?

The stone of *courage* will be essential to your victory. As we survey the challenges of life, we see that that which is easy is rarely right. In fact, the course which we should properly follow at times appears impossible, impenetrable, hopeless.

Such did the way appear to Laman and Lemuel. When they looked upon their assignment to go unto the house of Laban and seek the records according to God's command, they murmured, saying it was a hard thing which was required of them. Thus, a lack of courage took from them their opportunity, and it was given to courageous Nephi, who responded, "I will go and do the things which the Lord hath commanded, for I know that the Lord giveth no commandments unto the children of men, save he shall prepare a way for them that they may accomplish the thing which he commandeth them."[12] Yes, the stone of courage is needed.

Let us not overlook the stone of *effort*—both mental effort and physical effort.

> *The heights by great men reached and kept*
> *Were not attained by sudden flight,*
> *But they, while their companions slept,*
> *Were toiling upward in the night.*[13]

The decision to overcome a fault or correct a weakness is an actual step in the process of doing so. "Thrust in your sickles . . . with all your might"[14] was not spoken of missionary work alone.

There must also be in our selection the stone of *humility*. Haven't we been told through divine revelation that when we are humble, the Lord, our God, will lead us by the hand and give us answer to our prayers?[15]

And who would go forth to battle his Goliath without the stone of *prayer?* Remember that the recognition of a power higher than oneself is in no way debasing; rather, it exalts.

Finally, let us choose the stone of *duty*. Duty is not merely to do the thing we ought to do, but to do it when we should, whether we like it or not.

Armed with this selection of five polished stones to be propelled by the mighty sling of faith, we need then but to take the staff of virtue to steady us, and we are ready to meet the giant Goliath—wherever and whenever and however we find him.

The stone of *courage* will melt the Goliath of fear; the stone of *effort* will bring down the Goliaths of indecision and procrastination. And the Goliaths of pride, of envy, of lack of self-respect will not stand before the power of the stones of *humility, prayer,* and *duty.*

Above all else, may we ever remember that we do not go forth alone to battle against the Goliaths of our lives. As David declared to Israel, so might we echo the knowledge: "The battle is the Lord's, and he will give [Goliath] into our hands."[16]

The battle must be fought. Victory cannot come by default. So it is in the battles of life. Life will never spread itself in an unobstructed view before us. We must anticipate the approaching forks and turnings in the road.

However, we cannot hope to reach our desired journey's end if we think aimlessly about whether to go east or west. We must make our decisions purposefully. Our most significant opportunities will be found in times of greatest difficulty.

The vast, uncharted expanse of the Atlantic Ocean stood as a Goliath between Christopher Columbus and the new world. The hearts of his comrades became faint, their courage dimmed, and hopelessness engulfed them; but Columbus prevailed with his watchword, "Westward, ever westward, sail on, sail on."

Carthage Jail. An angry mob with painted faces. Certain death faced the Prophet Joseph Smith. But from the wellsprings of his abundant faith, he calmly met the Goliath of death. He had said, "I am going like a lamb to the slaughter; but I am calm as a summer's morning; I have a conscience void of offense towards God, and towards all men."[17]

Gethsemane. Golgotha. Intense pain and suffering beyond the comprehension of mortal man stood between Jesus the Master and victory over the grave. Yet He lovingly assured us, "I go to prepare a place for you . . . that where I am, there ye may be also."[18]

And what is the significance of these accounts? Had there been no ocean, there would have been no Columbus. No jail, no Joseph. No mob, no martyr. No cross, no Christ!

Should there be a Goliath in our lives or a giant called by any other name, we need not "flee" or be "sore afraid" as we go up to battle against him. Rather we can find assurance and divine help in that inspired psalm of David: "The Lord is my shepherd; I shall not want. . . . Yea, though I walk through the valley of the shadow of death, I will fear no evil: for thou art with me."[19]

May this knowledge be ours, I pray, in the name of Jesus Christ. Amen.

NOTES

This address was delivered by Elder Thomas S. Monson at the 137th Semiannual General Conference of The Church of Jesus Christ of Latter-day Saints, Salt Lake City, Utah, 1 October 1967.

1. 1 Samuel 17:8.
2. 1 Samuel 17:10.
3. 1 Samuel 17:24.
4. 1 Samuel 17:29, 32.
5. 1 Samuel 17:33.
6. 1 Samuel 17:40.
7. 1 Samuel 17:43–44.
8. 1 Samuel 17:45–47.
9. 1 Samuel 17:48–50.
10. 1 Samuel 18:7.
11. Alexander Pope, "An Essay on Man," Epistle 2, lines 217ff.
12. 1 Nephi 3:7.
13. Henry Wadsworth Longfellow, "The Ladder of Saint Augustine," stanza 10.
14. Doctrine and Covenants 33:7.
15. See Doctrine and Covenants 112:10.
16. 1 Samuel 17:47.
17. Doctrine and Covenants 135:4.
18. John 14:2–3.
19. Psalm 23:1, 4.